THE SELF-CARE SQUAD JOURNAL

THE SELF-CARE SQUAD JOURNAL

For Teens and Pre-teens

Amy Claire

VERITAS

Published 2021 by
Veritas Publications
7–8 Lower Abbey Street
Dublin 1, Ireland
publications@veritas.ie
www.veritas.ie

ISBN 978 1 84730 986 0

10 9 8 7 6 5 4 3 2 1

Design by Amy Claire Ford
Typeset by Padraig McCormack
Printed in Ireland by Watermans Printers, Cork

Veritas books are printed on paper made from the wood pulp of managed forests. For every tree felled, at least one tree is planted, thereby renewing natural resources.

CONTENTS

WHAT DO I NEED TO USE THIS JOURNAL?

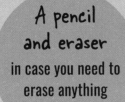

A pencil and eraser
in case you need to erase anything

An open mind
for all parts of this book

Colouring pens or markers
for mindfulness art

A mirror
for affirmations

But most of all your ...

Creativity

Imagination

This journal belongs to

....

You Are
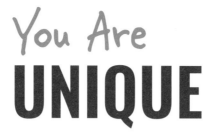

UNIQUE

If you are reading this, you are unique. There is only a one in 400 trillion chance of you actually being born. That's pretty unique! Of course, there will be similarities with loved ones but there is **no one else on this earth exactly like you** and **you are amazing**. This book will help you to start believing in yourself and all that you are and all that you can do!

Most parts of this book will be in the first person, using 'I am'. It is personal to you and you only. On the next page is your first I AM statement. So, you could read it and roll your eyes – or what if you actually believed it? And why wouldn't you?

It's a fact!

I Am
UNIQUE

When you see an I AM statement, read it quietly to yourself and then say it out loud five times, or three times in front of a mirror, and smile at your uniqueness.

I Am
UNIQUE
because ...

I CAN
and I AM

On the next page, jot down your abilities, skills and mannerisms; for example, *I am good at giving hugs, I am a good listener, I can help my friends with worries.*

A pencil is handy in case you need to erase anything and start again

I CAN

Abilities

I AM

Who you are

ACHIEVEMENTS LOG

For the next few weeks, you are going to log all of your wonderful achievements in your Achievements Log!

Everyone will have different achievements. No matter how big or small you think an achievement is – it goes into your log. Finishing your homework, listening to your friend, helping at home, not arguing with your siblings – it all goes in here!

My Weekly
ACHIEVEMENTS LOG

Week I

My Weekly
ACHIEVEMENTS LOG

Week 2

My Weekly
ACHIEVEMENTS LOG

Week 3

My Weekly
ACHIEVEMENTS LOG

Week 4

So many achievements! **Go you!** If you ever need motivation, just look at these and you will be on **FIRE!**

Do You Ever Get
COMPLIMENTS?

Do you think people are just being polite?

 # WELL, THAT
STOPS NOW!

This Compliments Log is where you write down things that people tell you; for example, 'You look nice today', 'That is great work', 'I love how you're so good at that!' These are compliments and a lot of the time, we don't believe them. But **now you will start to believe** them! The trick is to write down the compliment, then put it in your own words.

For example, 'Tonight, Jenny said I looked **beautiful** at the dance,' **transforms** into, '**I looked beautiful at the dance tonight and I felt great, I had a great time**.' Attach with the feeling and the belief that the compliment is true, because you know what?

It is true!

You Are
AMAZING

My Weekly
COMPLIMENTS LOG

First, you write the compliment, then put it in the first person I AM and write how it makes you feel.

Week 1

My Weekly
COMPLIMENTS LOG

Try to write compliment entries as you get them! They might be hard to remember at the end of the week.

Week 2

My Weekly
COMPLIMENTS LOG

Connect with how the compliment made you feel and why it made you feel that way; for example, 'The compliment made me feel really good because I didn't realise that was the case.'

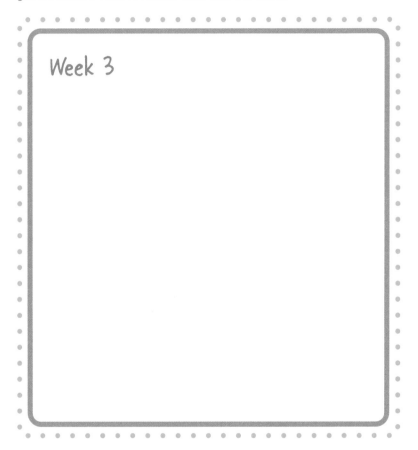

Week 3

My Weekly
COMPLIMENTS LOG

Self-Care Tip: Read the compliments back to yourself in the mirror! How amazing is it to believe what people tell you? The only thing that comes between you and believing the compliment is your thoughts. By changing the compliment to an I AM statement, we feel more powerful!

Week 4

MINDFULNESS

is about

Living in the Moment

Research has shown that mindfulness helps us reduce anxiety and depression.

Mindfulness teaches us how to respond to stress with awareness of what is happening in the present moment, rather than simply acting instinctively, unaware of what emotions or motives may be driving that decision.

Let's try to feel what we are feeling because we are human beings being human. You are human and unique!

When You Are Anxious
WHAT DO YOU FEEL? AND WHERE?

Mark with an ✗

MINDFULNESS

When you have the anxious feeling, try to become aware of the feeling, rather than trying to make it go away.

Breathe into it, no matter where it is – in your stomach or head or wherever you feel it – and allow it be for a moment. Then say to yourself:

☑ **This is normal**

☑ **This is temporary**

These affirmations can help.
If you are worried about anxiety, always talk to someone you trust or visit mentalhealth.ie.

☑ I AM CALM

☑ I AM RELAXED

☑ I AM OKAY

☑ I AM EXCITED

☑ I AM BRAVE

☑ I AM CAPABLE

☑ I AM AMAZING

☑ **YOU'RE DOING** *great!*

MINDFULNESS *Art*

 RELAXING

 SOOTHING

 CALMING

The next pages are for mindful colouring. Yes, you might think *I am not a child!* But, colouring is about being in the moment with yourself. Maybe listen to music and get out your favourite pens. You can get creative in this section. All that matters is here and now. These are great to do in a coffee shop, free class/period or whenever you need some relaxation. Mindful colouring is used in many countries for art therapy.

It is a type of art therapy you can do alone.

MINDFULNESS Art

Mandalas are geometric designs that symbolise the universe and the circle of life, showing us that we are all connected – to each other and to nature. A mandala is often used as a symbol to focus the mind during meditation and to create a sense of oneness with the universe.

Mandalas are used for art therapy because the repetition is soothing and shows the artist that repeated action and effort will bring results.

To make the most of this activity, find a quiet space, then begin. Notice how you feel as you are colouring. You can title the pieces; for example, 'Heartbreak', 'Love', 'Peace'.

Tip: Calming colours are purple, orange and blues

BELIEFS

Whether you think you
can or think you can't –
You're right!

POWER

You become what you
believe about yourself!

What do you believe to be true about yourself?

Let's explore this a little bit more ...

BELIEFS

There are many types of beliefs, but the two main ones that affect our lives are *limiting beliefs* and *empowering beliefs*.

Limiting Beliefs

They hold us back. Example:

* I have two left feet so I could never be good at dancing.

They are based on the past and are not real anymore. Example:

* I can't sing.
* I am not good at art.

You can stand in your own way by repeating limiting beliefs about yourself.

Empowering Beliefs

They are based on the present. They are true and real in this moment. They are positive and helpful. Examples of how to turn a limiting belief into an empowering belief:

* I can learn to sing in my own way!

* I enjoy art and I am trying to improve my drawing skills.

You can free yourself from these chains by being kind to YOU.

BELIEFS

Limiting Beliefs

We have control over what we can and can't do. We have natural skills and abilities, of course, but we can accept things by being gentle with ourselves.

We can change our *can'ts* into *cans* and our *won'ts* into *will dos*.

Empowering Beliefs

* I can do anything I set my mind to. ✓

* I have a lot of work to do but I will get through it piece by piece. ✓

* I am learning to be calm during conflict. ✓

* I am learning to be nice to myself when I do something wrong. ✓

BELIEFS

Here are some examples of how to turn limiting beliefs into empowering beliefs.

Limiting Beliefs

* I can't trust people because I've been betrayed before.

* I can't pursue my dreams because I don't know what I would do if I failed.

* I can't do A because of B.

* I can't do this because of that.

Empowering Beliefs

* I will learn to trust people in my own time.

* I want to pursue my dreams because I will never know what could be if I don't try.

* I will give this a try and see.

* It is not my job to please people in life.

* Today, I will just be myself. There'll never be anyone else like me.

BELIEFS

Think of some of your limiting beliefs and see how you can change them into empowering beliefs based on facts and the present moment.

Limiting Beliefs

*
*
*
*
*

Empowering Beliefs

*
*
*
*
*

BELIEFS

I AM Statements

List your empowering beliefs from the previous page and repeat them to yourself. All empowering beliefs start with a positive, such as, 'I am', 'I will', 'I am learning', 'I trust' or 'I love'.

*
*
*
*
*
*
*
*
*
*

BELIEFS

Empowering Life Lessons Photo

Add a photo of yourself on this page and write beside it something that you have learnt since the photo was taken.

 **Example:** This is me last summer. I had just had a fight with my friend. Since this photo was taken I have learnt to not let someone who makes me feel bad about myself be part of my life. I have new friends now who I trust.

If you don't have a photo, don't worry – you can draw yourself or just write down something you have learnt about yourself in the past year.

Squad
GOALS

The next few pages are for journalling your goals. Write down your goals on the next page and explore your options, assess your reality and make a decision about what you want to do by answering these questions for yourself.

Your Goal

» What do you want to get?
» What can you do about it today?
» What is the timescale?
» What would your goal look like if you achieved it?

Your Reality

» What is the current situation in detail?
» How strongly do you feel about the situation needing to change on a scale of one to ten?
» What have you done about it so far? What have been the outcomes of your efforts so far?
» What obstacles are in the way of getting what you really want?
» What help do you need to make this happen?
» Where will you get this help?
» What are the different ways you could approach this?

Options

» What options do you have?
» What could you do? What else?
» If there were no limitations, what would you do?
» What resources do you need?
» What are the advantages and disadvantages of these options?
» Which of these options appeals to you most?
» Which options would give you the most satisfaction?

Will Do

» What are you willing to do?
» How does this meet your objectives?
» How will you measure your success?
» What could stop you achieving this? Remember to be kind and flexible with yourself here.
» What support do you need? How will you get it?
» How will you overcome this?
» What are the key actions and what timescales do you have around these key actions? For example, 'In month one, I want to …'
» What is the next step now?

GROW

» **Goal**
» **Reality**
» **Options**
» **Will Do**

Squad
GOALS

Write down your goal, then explore your options, assess your reality and decide what you want to do.

My **GOAL IS:**

My **REALITY IS:**

My **OPTIONS ARE:**

WHAT I AM GOING to do:

Squad
GOALS

Write down your goal, then explore your options, assess your reality and decide what you want to do.

My **GOAL IS:**

My **REALITY IS:**

My **OPTIONS ARE:**

WHAT I AM GOING to do:

Squad
GOALS

Write down your goal, then explore your options, assess your reality and decide what you want to do.

My **GOAL IS:**

My **REALITY IS:**

My **OPTIONS ARE:**

WHAT I AM GOING *to do*:

Squad
GOALS

Write down your goal, then explore your options, assess your reality and decide what you want to do.

My **GOAL IS:**

My **REALITY IS:**

My **OPTIONS ARE:**

WHAT I AM GOING to do:

Squad
GOALS

Write down your goal, then explore your options, assess your reality and decide what you want to do.

My **GOAL IS:**

My **REALITY IS:**

My **OPTIONS ARE:**

WHAT I AM GOING to do:

Squad
GOALS

When you achieve any of these goals make sure to include them in your *Achievements Log*.

Write down your goal, then explore your options, assess your reality and decide what you want to do.

My **GOAL IS:**

My **REALITY IS:**

My **OPTIONS ARE:**

WHAT I AM GOING *to do*:

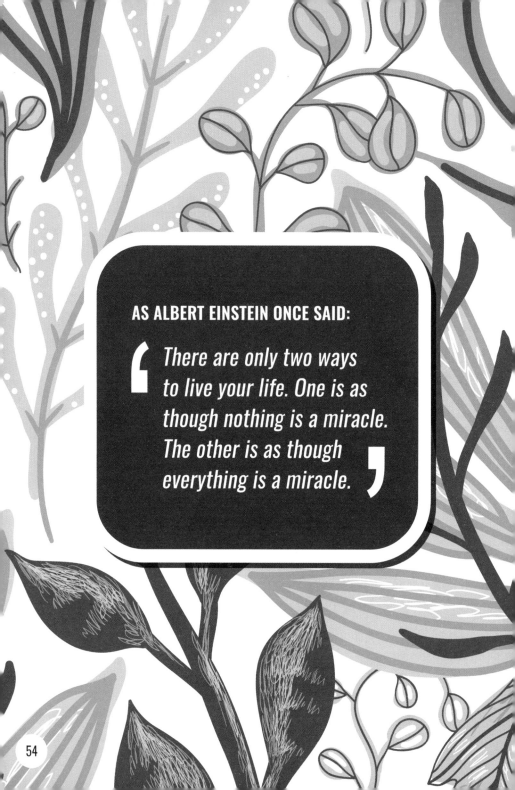

AS ALBERT EINSTEIN ONCE SAID:

There are only two ways to live your life. One is as though nothing is a miracle. The other is as though everything is a miracle.

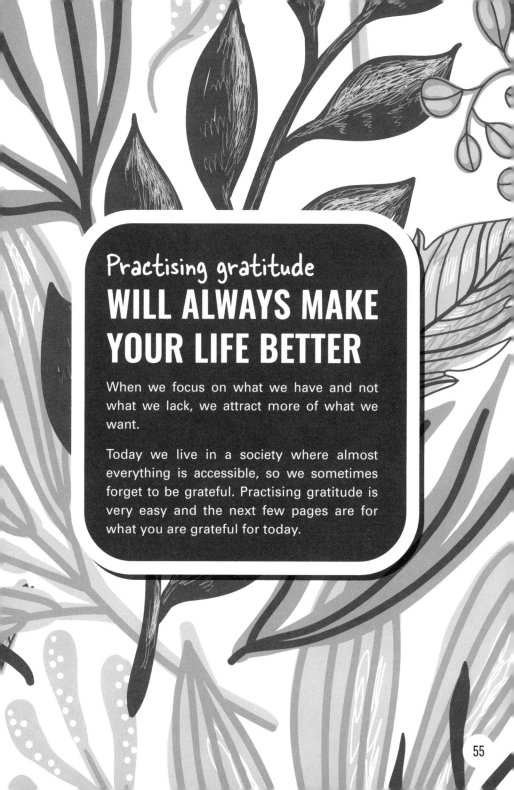

Practising gratitude
WILL ALWAYS MAKE YOUR LIFE BETTER

When we focus on what we have and not what we lack, we attract more of what we want.

Today we live in a society where almost everything is accessible, so we sometimes forget to be grateful. Practising gratitude is very easy and the next few pages are for what you are grateful for today.

Today, I am grateful for ...

1.

2.

3.

4.

5.

Example:

    1. My cosy bed. 2. My friends.
    3. My phone. 4. The sunshine.

KEEP IT SIMPLE

Today, I am grateful for ...

1.

2.

3.

4.

5.

Today, I am grateful for ...

1.

2.

3.

4.

5.

Today, I am grateful for ...

1.

2.

3.

4.

5.

Today, I am grateful for ...

1.

2.

3.

4.

5.

Today, I am grateful for ...

1.

2.

3.

4.

5.

Today, I am grateful for ...

1.

2.

3.

4.

5.

Today, I am grateful for ...

1.

2.

3.

4.

5.

Today, I am grateful for ...

1.

2.

3.

4.

5.

Today, I am grateful for ...

1.

2.

3.

4.

5.

Affirmations

All the affirmations you will ever need!

Affirmations are a very powerful addition to your day and can become a healthy habit. This section gives you a selection of affirmations based around different intentions. These affirmations can be used as tools to move towards your intentions. When you find an affirmation that suits your intention, read it aloud and repeat it to yourself over the course of each day.

 Part one is for **stability**. It has affirmations and statements for courage, patience, responsibility, independence, self-sufficiency and instinct.

 Part two is for **well-being**. It has affirmations and statements for emotions, health, abundance, reward, personal power and optimism.

 Part three is for **confidence** and self-worth. It has affirmations and statements for inner harmony, self-esteem, strength, self-confidence and empathy.

 Part four is for **compassion**. It has affirmations and statements for forgiveness, compassion, sincerity, self-acceptance, peace, unconditional love and generosity.

 Part five is for **expression**. It has affirmations and statements for expressing feelings, communication, creative expression and setting boundaries.

 Part six is for **wisdom**. It has affirmations and statements for imagination, mindfulness and knowledge.

Affirmations for
STABILITY

1

Finding stability can be fantastic for feeling grounded and feeling like you have two feet on the ground. Feeling balanced is a choice. Often you can feel thrown off balance by your day-to-day life, so practising stability affirmations is a great way to plant yourself back on solid ground.

Find the affirmation or affirmations that suit you best and learn them, so they become part of your day.

1. Courage

2. Patience

3. Responsibility

4. Independence

5. Self-sufficiency

6. Instinct

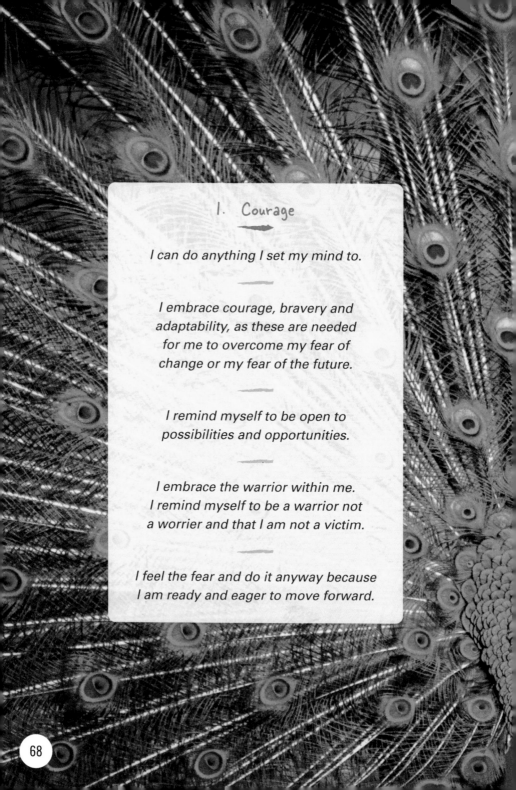

1. Courage

I can do anything I set my mind to.

I embrace courage, bravery and adaptability, as these are needed for me to overcome my fear of change or my fear of the future.

I remind myself to be open to possibilities and opportunities.

I embrace the warrior within me. I remind myself to be a warrior not a worrier and that I am not a victim.

I feel the fear and do it anyway because I am ready and eager to move forward.

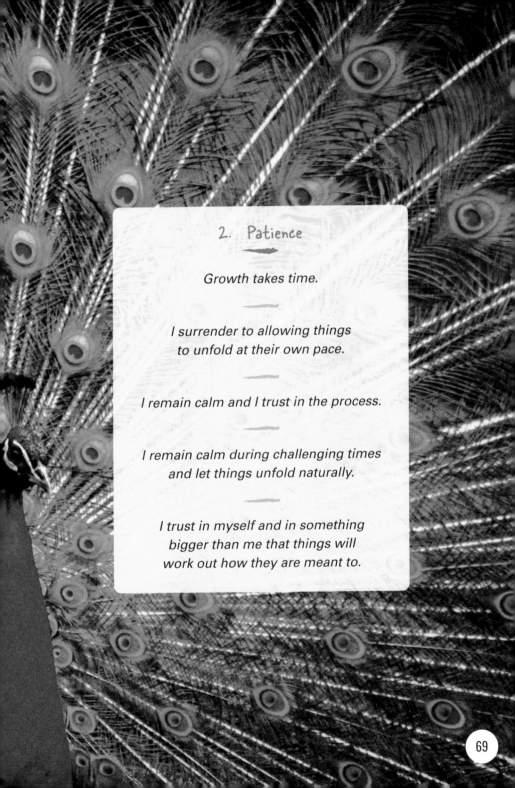

2. Patience

Growth takes time.

*I surrender to allowing things
to unfold at their own pace.*

I remain calm and I trust in the process.

*I remain calm during challenging times
and let things unfold naturally.*

*I trust in myself and in something
bigger than me that things will
work out how they are meant to.*

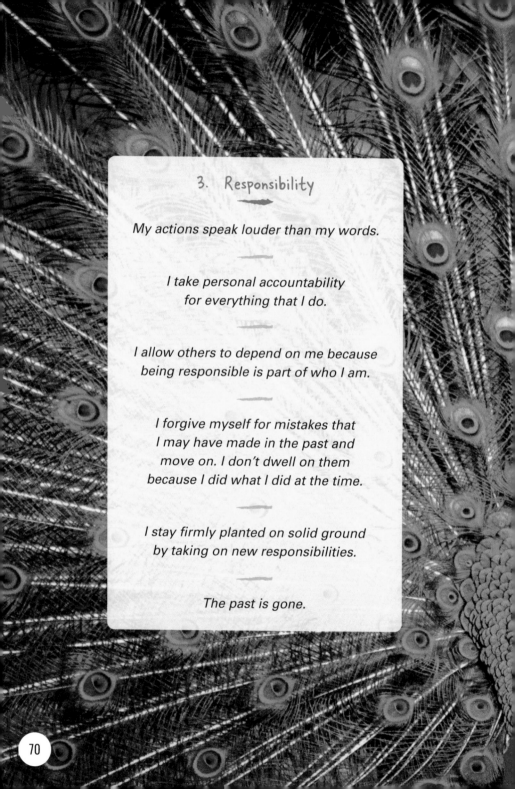

3. Responsibility

My actions speak louder than my words.

I take personal accountability
for everything that I do.

I allow others to depend on me because
being responsible is part of who I am.

I forgive myself for mistakes that
I may have made in the past and
move on. I don't dwell on them
because I did what I did at the time.

I stay firmly planted on solid ground
by taking on new responsibilities.

The past is gone.

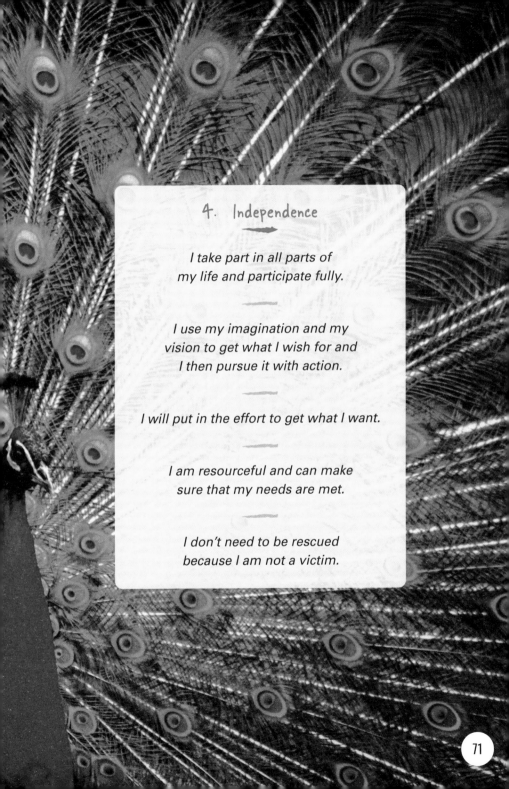

4. Independence

*I take part in all parts of
my life and participate fully.*

*I use my imagination and my
vision to get what I wish for and
I then pursue it with action.*

I will put in the effort to get what I want.

*I am resourceful and can make
sure that my needs are met.*

*I don't need to be rescued
because I am not a victim.*

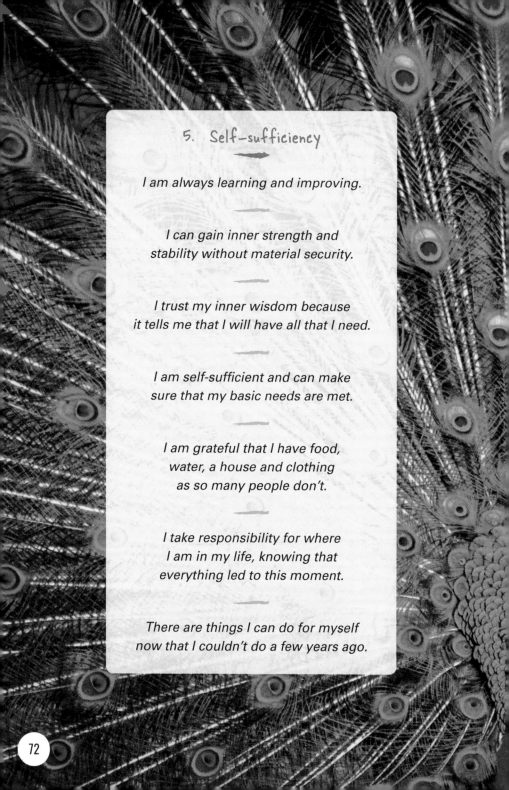

5. Self-sufficiency

I am always learning and improving.

*I can gain inner strength and
stability without material security.*

*I trust my inner wisdom because
it tells me that I will have all that I need.*

*I am self-sufficient and can make
sure that my basic needs are met.*

*I am grateful that I have food,
water, a house and clothing
as so many people don't.*

*I take responsibility for where
I am in my life, knowing that
everything led to this moment.*

*There are things I can do for myself
now that I couldn't do a few years ago.*

6. Instinct

I trust in my own instincts and
I know they are there to protect me.

I trust my gut feeling but also question
where the instinct comes from.

I respond with wisdom when
situations come my way.

I believe in myself.

I know that I am destined for
great things and I look out for
clues in the world around me.

I choose to respond rather
than react to situations.

My instincts are there for a reason. If
I don't feel safe I will say so and tell
someone that I don't feel safe.

I am wise.

Affirmations for
WELL-BEING

Staying in the moment and really feeling your feelings can be great for growth as well as overall positivity and well-being. Practise these affirmations when you are feeling low on energy and they will work like a charm!

Find the affirmation or affirmations that suit you best and repeat them over the course of each day, so they become part of your day.

1. Emotions

2. Health

3. Abundance

4. Reward

5. Personal Power

6. Optimism

1. Emotions

I encourage myself to express my emotions and allow my emotions to come without judgement.

———

I practise being aware of my emotions in the morning and I allow myself to feel them.

———

Whatever way I feel today is okay. I am right where I need to be.

———

If I need to cry, I am not ashamed. It is my body's way of releasing feelings.

———

I don't try to force myself to feel happy. I feel how I feel and it is temporary. Feelings will always change and I allow them to.

———

I am only human.

2. Health

*I respect my body and I feed it
with nourishing, healthy food.*

---

*I feed my brain with healthy thoughts
and beliefs because my mind will
believe anything that I tell it.*

---

*I allow myself to relax and be still
if I am tired or need to recharge.*

I go gently with myself.

---

*My body deserves the best
nourishing food to keep it healthy.*

---

*I try to only eat and drink foods that
are designed to nourish me because
I know that my food will affect
how I behave, feel and think.*

---

*I like to move to keep my energy
moving in my body and to keep
the blood flowing.*

---

*Exercise is good for my
body and my mind.*

3. Abundance

I am worthy and I deserve abundance.

To make sure that I am respecting myself I watch my thoughts to make sure they are positive and helpful for my life.

I am worthy to receive nice things and my basic needs will always be met.

The more I am grateful for what I have, the more I will get.

I know that when I ask for help it is a sign of strength and not a weakness.

I live an abundant life and I can attract good things into my life by being grateful for what I do have and not focusing on what I don't have.

I am open to new experiences and environments.

4. Reward

*I know that I deserve good things
in life so I give myself
permission to have them.*

———

*I work hard and acknowledge the
work that I do by treating myself.*

———

*I try not to exhaust myself with too much
work and very little play. I know that I
must have a balance.*

———

*I am flexible and open to change.
Sometimes I don't acknowledge my
efforts but now I pat myself on the
back and tell myself 'GO ME!'*

———

*I embrace new things and activities
even when I may have avoided
them in the past.*

———

*I realise that I deserve fun and I embrace
new fun things where I will be safe.*

———

*I am open to new ways
of rewarding myself.*

5. Personal Power

I choose to be myself
and to express myself.

———

I do not allow my personal
power to be led by my ego.

———

I don't use my personal power to
manipulate or exploit. I use my personal
power for good and for kindness.

———

I allow my confidence to shine,
which makes me more confident.
When I am confident I can do
anything and encourage others.

———

I know that I have a powerful
presence and people feel my energy
and it makes their day better.

———

I choose to always try to have
a positive influence on situations
and environments and the
people around me.

6. Optimism

*I use my optimism to see the
good in situations that could
be seen as bad situations.*

———

*I see problems as an opportunity
to learn and grow and do something.*

———

*I face setbacks with patience and
calmness, knowing that it will all pass.*

———

*I use my inner wisdom and confidence
to trust my gut that things will work out.
When bad things happen, I tell myself
that this is part of life and it will be okay.*

———

I will always be okay.

———

*I am kind to myself and I know that
solutions will lead to positivity.*

Affirmations for
CONFIDENCE

3

What does it look like when you are confident? Are you glowing? Are you on top of the world? Well – here are more affirmations to make you feel even more awesome!

Find the affirmation or affirmations that suit you best and repeat them over the course of each day, so they become part of your day.

1. Inner Harmony

2. Self-esteem

3. Strength

4. Self-confidence

5. Empathy

1. Inner Harmony

If you are not at peace with yourself, you might find it hard to be at peace in different situations and in the world. Real change happens on the inside when you accept all parts of yourself and love yourself. These affirmations can help you with inner harmony.

I do not allow my mind to create doubt or talk over my gut feelings.

I accept and express my feelings while I still accept the feelings of others and respect them.

I am at peace with myself and those around me and I don't have unrealistic expectations of myself or others.

I am free from ego and I trust myself completely, knowing that I will do the right thing.

2. Self-esteem

Self-esteem is knowing that you don't always have to please everyone. You can't people-please all the time. Self-esteem is about honouring and knowing yourself in order to equip yourself and please yourself.

When I respect and approve of myself, others will naturally do the same.

I teach others how to treat me by how I treat myself.

I am worthy of love and respect and I love and respect myself.

I empower myself by reminding myself that I don't need to live up to unrealistic expectations of myself.

The boundaries that I create acknowledge my self-worth.

3. Strength

Being strong can take time but being strong is a state as well as a process. You are only as strong as you tell yourself that you are and you grow stronger by trusting yourself and not holding yourself back.

I trust myself to not hold myself back from doing what I am here to do.

I embrace my inner strength and my power and I keep shining.

I empower myself by overcoming challenges and obstacles.

I am courageous and moving forward, knowing that I am a warrior not a victim.

I am an empowered person with a true sense of who I really am and that is strong.

4. Self-confidence

Try these affirmations before an exam or in some other situation where you may not feel confident. Stand with your hands on your hips, stand tall and say them out loud – even better if it's in a mirror.

I fully trust myself.

Fear does not hold me back.

Fear stands for Fantasised Experiences Appearing Real.

I have confidence, belief and conviction in my goals.

I welcome questions from others as it gives me a chance to clarify my ideas.

I stand up tall and am open to new challenges.

5. Empathy

I see everything as part of my life by accepting others for who they are.

I respond with empathy; for example, 'I am sorry that is happening to you.' I don't try to fix the problems of others – that is not my responsibility.

I let myself be supported by others.

I choose to see kindness when I look around me.

I accept everyone and don't try to change anyone.

I find common ground with others rather than differences.

I get on well with everyone because I see the similarities and not the groups or gangs or titles – I see that we are all human.

4 Affirmations for
COMPASSION

Compassion is a positive emotion, centred on kindness. It is about being kind, loving, thoughtful and decent with yourself and with others.

Find the affirmation or affirmations that suit you best and repeat them over the course of each day, so they become part of your day.

1. Forgiveness

2. Compassion

3. Sincerity

4. Self-acceptance

5. Peace

6. Unconditional Love

7. Generosity

1. Forgiveness

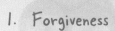

*I forgive those around
me for their mistakes.*

---

*I let go of anger, resentment and
regrets from the past and I forgive
myself with love and kindness.*

I give myself the gift of forgiveness.

---

*There are things I could have done
differently in the past but I remind
myself that my response was what
it was at that time and it's over.*

---

*I listen, understand and share
with others and forgive myself
for days when I am less patient.*

---

*Forgiveness happens on the inside so I
forgive people who have wronged me in
the past because I have learnt from it.*

2. Compassion

*I show respect and kindness
to those around me.*

*I act with dignity when
something goes wrong.*

*I allow my inner doubts to be
acknowledged and I observe
them but don't believe them.*

*I show kindness and love
to animals and nature.*

*I understand that my body is
a gift and needs to be nourished.
I give my brain and body healthy
thoughts and healthy food.*

*I have an open heart and I acknowledge
people's feelings by showing I care.*

3. Sincerity

A smile or a hug can uplift many
and it really goes a long way
when it is heartfelt and sincere.

I smile at people when I see
them because smiles are
contagious, just like a yawn.

I offer care and support where
and when I can, without rescuing.

It is not my responsibility
to rescue anyone.

I nurture and respect my relationships.

I don't lie about things because
that is being insincere towards
myself and others.

4. Self-acceptance
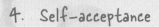

*I give myself love and accept
myself the way that I am.*

———

*I know that to compare is to despair
and I don't compare myself to others.*

———

*I focus on what is right in my life,
not what is wrong.*

———

*I move forwards from here and accept
where I am right here and right now.*

———

*I feel great about my life and I do this by
feeling great about myself and forgiving
myself and loving myself and being
compassionate with myself.*

———

*I am the way that I am
and that is beautiful.*

5. Peace

I am peaceful and calm.

Peace is a part of my life.

I make time to be peaceful every day.

*Peace brings me calmness and brings
me into the moment.*

*I trust that everything will work out and
I don't take on more than I can handle.*

*When I feel good about myself, have
self-acceptance and self-compassion, it
will bring more peace into my life.*

6. Unconditional Love

*I always show respect
and kindness to myself.*

*I allow myself to be open without
a fear of rejection of me or my ideas.*

*I love myself the way that I am, not
how I used to be or could be or should
be – but as I am right now. I extend
this love to others.*

*I teach others how to love
and respect me by how I show
love and respect to myself.*

*I give love without expecting
recognition or acknowledgement.*

I love and respect myself.

7. Generosity

Generosity is sharing of love, kindness and spirit.

I am open to opportunities to give myself freely when I can.

I speak from the heart. Through generosity of spirit I help other people and have an impact on their lives.

I trust my gut and am generous to those I love.

I am kind by showing affection and appreciation for the gifts I have and the skills that I have.

I share without needing anything in return.

5 Affirmations for
EXPRESSION

How we express ourselves and communicate must be in line with who we are as people and support our confidence, compassion and kindness to ourselves. These affirmations are great for working on your communication as well as setting boundaries and expressing yourself creatively.

Find the affirmation or affirmations that suit you best and repeat them over the course of each day, so they become part of your day.

1. Expressing Feelings

2. Communication

3. Creative Expression

4. Setting Boundaries

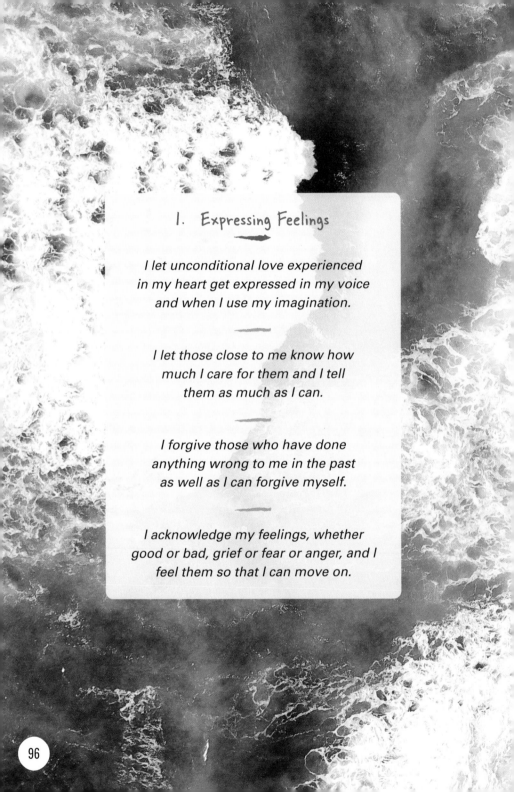

I. Expressing Feelings

*I let unconditional love experienced
in my heart get expressed in my voice
and when I use my imagination.*

*I let those close to me know how
much I care for them and I tell
them as much as I can.*

*I forgive those who have done
anything wrong to me in the past
as well as I can forgive myself.*

*I acknowledge my feelings, whether
good or bad, grief or fear or anger, and I
feel them so that I can move on.*

2. Communication

I am open to giving and receiving praise and I make space for people to give me praise and communicate with me.

I want to be fully understood by others and I express how I feel openly and without fear.

I ask how other people are doing and I respond honestly when asked how I am feeling.

I am clear when I speak because my voice is important.

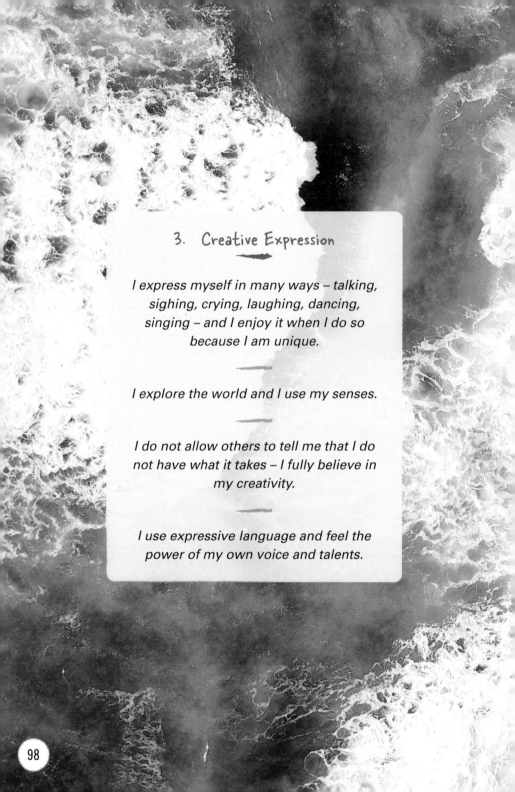

3. Creative Expression

I express myself in many ways – talking, sighing, crying, laughing, dancing, singing – and I enjoy it when I do so because I am unique.

I explore the world and I use my senses.

I do not allow others to tell me that I do not have what it takes – I fully believe in my creativity.

I use expressive language and feel the power of my own voice and talents.

4. Setting Boundaries

*I speak up for myself and I expect
respect, patience, tolerance and support.*

*I teach people how to love and respect
me by how I love and respect myself.*

*I have the right to say no and when
I say no to one thing I say yes to
something else that is more important.*

*I do not allow myself to feel guilt
because guilt is the result of causing
intentional harm. I will not feel guilt
if I don't feel like doing something
that isn't important to me.*

6 Affirmations for
WISDOM

Dolphins are known as the wisest animals on earth. They could teach us a few things about wisdom! Unfortunately, they can be difficult to understand so these affirmations will help you to become more worldly wise.

Find the affirmation or affirmations that suit you best and repeat them over the course of each day, so they become part of your day.

1. Imagination

2. Mindfulness

3. Knowledge

1. Imagination

*I imagine my life when
I have all that I want.*

My thoughts create my reality.

I respect my dreams and wishes.

My imagination is important.

*I encourage myself to
use my imagination.*

2. Mindfulness

I am aware of my thinking and my thoughts and I ask myself if these thoughts are making me feel good or making me feel bad. If a thought makes me feel good, I will remind myself of that thought when I feel bad. When I feel bad I will be inquisitive as to why I feel bad and forgive myself.

———

I am not in control of everything in the world but I am in control of my responses and thoughts about things.

———

I allow myself to sit with myself without judgement.

———

My body will believe what I tell it so I tell it nice things like I am able, I am worthy, I am loved.

3. Knowledge

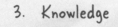

*My knowledge comes to me
in my intuition and I trust
my knowledge and share it.*

———

*I have faith in my knowledge
and use it with wisdom.*

———

*I aim to understand the truth
and I don't judge the information.
I simply observe.*

———

*My knowledge of myself is
always increasing and I use my
wisdom to tackle tough situations.*

FEEL-GOOD FOODS

For Your Body and Mind

FEEL-GOOD FOODS

For Your Body and Mind

BLUEBERRIES

» Great for your skin, hair and nails

» Full of Vitamin C and Vitamin K

TASTY AND SWEET
Great with yogurt or cereal

FEEL-GOOD FOODS

For Your Body and Mind

EGGS

» Great for your skin, hair
  and nails

» Super source of protein

VERSATILE

Scrambled, fried or an omelette

FEEL-GOOD FOODS

For Your Body and Mind

WHOLE GRAINS

» Brown rice, oats, popcorn

» Decrease risk of heart disease, great for fibre

OATS ARE GREAT WITH BLUEBERRIES

and vanilla yogurt

FEEL-GOOD FOODS

For Your Body and Mind

REMEMBER

» When you eat you are not only eating to not feel hungry, you are fuelling your body and your mind

BALANCE IS EVERYTHING

Be kind to your body

YOUR DIARY

One line a day:

› Thoughts
› Feelings
› Ideas
› New learnings
› New experiences
› New friends
› Emotions
› Dreams
› Wishes
› Hopes
› Aspirations
› Research

Whatever you wish!

IT'S YOURS!

> I let myself be as I am today without apologies. It felt amazing! Go me!
>
> Date: 01/05/21

DIARY

One line a day – thoughts and feelings

DIARY

One line a day – thoughts and feelings

DIARY

One line a day – thoughts and feelings

DIARY

One line a day – thoughts and feelings

DIARY

One line a day – thoughts and feelings

DIARY

One line a day – thoughts and feelings

DIARY

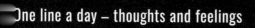

One line a day – thoughts and feelings

DIARY

One line a day – thoughts and feelings

DIARY

One line a day – thoughts and feelings

DIARY

One line a day — thoughts and feelings

DIARY

One line a day – thoughts and feelings

DIARY

One line a day – thoughts and feelings

_____

_____

_____

_____

_____

_____

_____

_____

_____

_____

_____

_____

_____

_____

_____

_____

_____

_____

_____

_____

_____

_____

_____

DIARY

One line a day – thoughts and feelings

DIARY

One line a day – thoughts and feelings

DIARY

One line a day – thoughts and feelings

One line a day – thoughts and feelings

_____

_____

_____

_____

_____

_____

_____

_____

_____

_____

_____

_____

_____

_____

_____

_____

_____

_____

_____

DIARY

One line a day – thoughts and feelings

DIARY

One line a day – thoughts and feelings

DIARY

One line a day – thoughts and feelings

DIARY

One line a day – thoughts and feelings

DIARY

More detailed world domination plans go here

DIARY

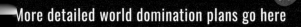

More detailed world domination plans go here

DIARY

More detailed world domination plans go here

_____
_____
_____
_____
_____
_____
_____
_____
_____
_____
_____
_____
_____
_____
_____
_____
_____

DIARY

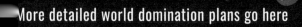

More detailed world domination plans go here

_____

_____

_____

_____

_____

_____

_____

_____

_____

_____

_____

_____

_____

_____

_____

_____

_____

_____

More detailed world domination plans go here

DIARY

More detailed world domination plans go here

DIARY

More detailed world domination plans go here

DIARY

More detailed world domination plans go here

DIARY

More detailed world domination plans go here

DIARY

More detailed world domination plans go here

DIARY

More detailed world domination plans go here

BULLET JOURNAL

For Whatever You Wish

Use your creativity and skills to draw, paint, write, design ...

It's up to you –

GO WILD!

To do

145

161

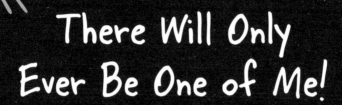

There Will Only Ever Be One of Me!

I am going to make the best life for myself
and remember that I deserve kindness,
love, support and nice things because

I am
AMAZING

and
no one has permission
to tell me otherwise.

THE END

(of this book)

but the beginning of your new mindful life ...

Take the Next Step

You have started the journey towards a mindful, peaceful and meaningful life. I wish you every success and although it is the end of the journey with this book, you will always have it and it is here for you to look at to remind yourself of all the hard work that you have done to invest in yourself. Remember, every day is a new day. The past is gone and all that matters is right here and right now. Give yourself permission to be nice to yourself, be kind to yourself and others. Have confidence in yourself that you are exactly where you need to be. Keep using your talents and believe in yourself.

Lots of love and hugs,

Amy Claire

A LITTLE BIT ABOUT THE AUTHOR

Amy Claire Ford is a qualified personal development coach and mentor to all age groups internationally and locally.

She has a background in career and confidence coaching in competitive industries. Amy has a BA in product design and business, is a published author and firm believer in positive and healthy living.

Amy would like to connect with herself as a teenager so that she could have been equipped at a young age to deal with life's challenges.

Amy's motto on life is:

We are whatever we feed ourselves, both mentally and physically – if we eat, think and act negatively or see ourselves as a victim, we will receive negative things in return. Being kind and patient with ourselves is something that we have full control over. We cannot control the world outside – but we most definitely can control our reactions and thoughts around things that happen, and live and love ourselves responsibly. Living in the here and now is all that counts and the past is gone – there is no point in revisiting the past because there is nothing new to find there.

Amy hopes this book brings value and clarity to teens, pre-teens and anyone that feels that they are in need of some mindful self-care.

Enjoy the book with an open mind and an open heart.

If you wish to contact Amy, she can be found at:

✉ **Email:** amy@thecoachingprogram.ie

📷 **Instagram:** @thecoachingprogram

ⓕ **Facebook:** @thecoachingprogram